AFFIRMATIONS AND PRAYERS

Affirmations & Prayers

by
J. DONALD WALTERS

CRYSTAL CLARITY

PUBLISHERS
14618 TYLER FOOTE ROAD
NEVADA CITY, CA 95959
(916) 292-3482 (CA only)
(800) 545-7475

Cover Design by Bella Potapovskaya

Copyright 1988 by J. Donald Walters

4th Printing, 1990

International Book Number 0-916124-45-2
Printed in the United States of America

To my spiritual family,
with all love.

CONTENTS

INTRODUCTION

The thoughts in this book are those by which I have tried to live my life. They are the fruit of experience, not of book learning. They represent lessons learned – sometimes in sorrow, disappointment, and pain; at other times, in the thrill of discovery and of expanding joy. Sometimes I have quoted the wise words of my spiritual teacher, for it might also be said that none of this book could have been written, had it not been for the guidance that I received from him.

There are fifty-two basic subjects covered. Thus, they can be used for every week of the year. But again, if you prefer, you can meditate on the qualities that are the most meaningful to you, turning to them at times of special need.

AFFIRMATION
AND PRAYER

An affirmation is a statement of truth which one aspires to absorb into his life. It has been said that we are what we eat. It would be truer to say, "We are what we think." For our minds express, and also influence, the reality of what we are far more than our bodies do. Our thoughts even influence, to a great extent, our physical health.

No real progress in life ever comes haphazardly. A sportsman must work hard to master the techniques he needs: throwing a ball, skiing down a difficult slope, jumping the greatest possible distance. And a pianist must work at least as hard to master the movements of his fingers, to play with ease the most intricate musical passages.

Living, too, is an art. Unfortunately, it is one to which most people devote little energy. They take life as it comes, and wonder why things keep going wrong.

Thoughts are things. Words, which are crystallized thoughts, have immeasurable power, especially when we speak them with concentration. The mere thought of fatigue is enough to sap our energy. To strengthen that thought by the words, "I'm exhausted," gives definition, and therefore added power, to the thought itself.

The opposite is true also. If one feels exhausted, but suddenly finds his interest drawn to something, his fatigue may vanish altogether! One *is* what one thinks. If, in addition to that sudden interest, he verbalizes it with the words, "I feel *wonderful!*" he may find that, instead of only feeling vaguely better, he actually feels as though he had acquired a new self-definition.

So many of our failures in life — to master new languages, to get along with others, to do well whatever we want to do — are due to the simple thought that what we want to accomplish is alien to us.

Again, many of our successes in life are the result of fully accepting the new as our own. French, for example, can be learned more easily by the student who absorbs himself in the thought, "I am French," than by him who says (as children in the classroom often do), "Those people talk *funny!*"

The difficulty is that our habits are buried in the subconscious mind. Thus, even when we resolve to change them, we find ourselves being drawn back repeatedly, and quite against our conscious will, into old ways.

Affirmations, on the other hand, when

repeated with deep concentration, then carried into the subconscious, can change us on levels of the mind over which most of us have little conscious control.

We are what we think. But we are also far more than what we think consciously. We are the myriad conflicting patterns of feeling, habit, and reaction that we have built up over a lifetime — indeed, over lifetimes — in our subconscious minds. To change our lives, we must also set those inner conflicts in order.

Nor is it enough, even, to affirm change on conscious and subconscious levels. For we are part of a much greater reality, with which we must live in harmony also. Behind our human minds is the divine consciousness.

When we try to transform ourselves by self-effort alone, we limit our potential for change. Affirmation should be lifted from the self-enclosure of the mind into the greater reality of superconsciousness.

The superconscious is that level of awareness which is often described as the higher Self. It is from this level, for example, that great inspirations come. It is through the superconscious that divine guidance descends. Without superconscious attunement, affirmations, like any other merely human attempt at self-upliftment, have only temporary benefits.

Affirmations should be repeated in such a way as to lift the consciousness toward superconsciousness. This they can accomplish when we repeat them with deep concentration at the seat of divine awareness in the human body, the Christ center, which is a point in the forehead midway between the two eyebrows.

Repeat the affirmations in this book loudly at first, to command the full attention of your conscious mind. Then repeat them quietly, to absorb more deeply the meaning of the words. Then speak them in a whisper, carrying their meaning down into the sub-conscious. Repeat them again, silently, to deepen your absorption of them at the sub-conscious level. Then at last, with rising aspiration, repeat them at the Christ center.

At every level, repeat them several times, absorbing yourself ever-more-deeply in their meaning.

By repeated affirmation you can strengthen, and, later, spiritualize your awareness of any quality you want to develop.

Affirmation is only the first step to self-perfection. We must do our human part. Without additional power from God, however, our efforts are forever incomplete. Affirmation, in other words, should end with prayer.

Why should one pray only after repeating the affirmations? Why not before? Prayer is always good, certainly. But if it isn't uttered with an affirmative consciousness, it can easily become weak and beggarly: a plea that God do all the work, without man's active participation. Effective prayer is never passive. It is full of faith. It matures in an attitude of affirmation.

To become established in any new quality, it helps first to affirm it, following the sequence that I have described. Then, however, offer that affirmation up in loving prayer to God.

It is at the point of our deepest and most positive attunement with Him that He helps us the most. By divine attunement, our resistance becomes minimized, and our cooperation with His grace becomes fully open, willing, and superconsciously aware.

1. SUCCESS

TRUE SUCCESS means transcendence. It means finding what we *really* want, which is not outward things, but inner peace of mind, self-understanding — and, above all, the joy of God.

Outward success means transcendence also. It means rising above past accomplishments to reach new levels of achievement. Success can mean accepting failure, too, when such acceptance helps us to transcend a false ambition. Every failure, moreover, can be a stepping stone to highest achievement.

Success should not be measured by the things accomplished, but by our increasing understanding, ability, and closeness to God.

Affirmation

I leave behind me both my failures and accomplishments. What I do today will create a new and better future, filled with inner joy.

≈

Prayer

O Creator of galaxies and countless, blazing stars, the power of the very universe is Thine! May I reflect that power in the little mirror of my life and consciousness.

2. LOVE

ONE FINDS LOVE not by *being* loved, but by loving.

We can never know love if we try to draw others to ourselves; nor can we find it by centering our love in them. For love is infinite; it is never ours to create. We can only channel it from its source in Infinity to all whom we meet.

The more we forget ourselves in giving to others, the better we can understand what love really is. And the more we love as channels for God's love, the more we can understand that His is the one love in all the universe.

Affirmation

I will love others as extensions of my own Self, and of the love I feel from God.

❧

Prayer

O Infinite One, make me a channel for Thy love! Through me, reach out to sow seeds of love in barren hearts everywhere.

3. HAPPINESS

HAPPINESS is an attitude of mind, born of the simple determination to *be* happy under all outward circumstances. Happiness lies not in things, nor in outward attainments. It is the gold of our inner nature, buried beneath the mud of outward sense-cravings.

When you know that nothing outside you can affect you — no disappointment, no failure, no misunderstanding from others — then you will know that you have found true happiness.

Resolve strongly to keep this flame burning ever in your heart.

Affirmation

I vow from today onwards to be happy under every circumstance. I came from God's joy. I *am* joy!

ঌ

Prayer

O Lord of Joy, fill me with boundless happiness. For I am Thy child, made in Thy blissful image. As Thou art Joy, so also, in my inner self, am I.

4. ENERGY

ENERGY IS OURS not when we hoard our strength, but when we devote it willingly, joyously toward the attainment of that in which we deeply believe.

Faith and energy go hand in hand. If you have deep faith in what you are doing, you can move mountains. Energy is always highest when one's cause is just. The greater one's faith, the greater his will power. And the greater his will power, the greater his flow of energy.

Affirmation

Within me lies the energy to accomplish all that I will to do. Behind my every act is God's infinite power.

❧

Prayer

O Cosmic Energy, vitalize all the cells of my body; recharge my mind with boundless inspiration; fill my soul with Thy inexhaustible joy.

5. SHARING

TRUE HAPPINESS is found not in possessions, but in sharing what one has with others. Thus is one's self-identity expanded, as he learns to live in, and enjoy, a greater reality.

People who gladly share with others feel themselves bathed by a constant, inner stream of happiness.

Sharing is the doorway through which the soul escapes the prison of self-preoccupation. It is one of the clearest paths to God.

Affirmation

What I give to others I give not away, for in my larger reality it remains ever mine. I am happy in the happiness of all!

Prayer

O Infinite Giver, teach me to find happiness through others.

6. WORK

WORK SHOULD BE done with a creative attitude — never for the sake of selfish gain, but for the chance it gives us to help create a better world.

Those who work with the thought of pay live in the future; they lose the habit of living here and now, where alone true happiness can be found.

Work should always be done as well as possible—not out of self-conceit, but in gratitude for the free gift of life, of sunshine, of water, of air — and in gratitude, simply, for our God-given power to be useful to our fellowman.

Affirmation

I will do my work thinking of Thee, Lord. I offer to Thee the very best that is in me.

৯

Prayer

Beloved Lord, who so wonderfully created the high, snowy mountains; the bounding rivers; the colorful, fragrant flowers; the vast, heaving oceans; and the distant, glittering stars: Manifest, through me, Thy perfect joy.

7. SECURITY

MAN STRUGGLES all his life to store up treasures for himself, to insure his property against loss and his health against the devastations of disease. He rests his faith in outward measures, and sees not that such faith is like asking a wave not to move!

Security is his alone whose faith rests in the Lord. Most practical of men is he who offers his life to God, praying, "My safety is Thy responsibility, Lord." This does not mean we should not be conscientious. But after doing our very best, we should leave the worrying to God!

Affirmation

I live in the fortress of God's inner presence.
Nothing and no one can break through these
walls and harm me.

≥

Prayer

I accept whatever comes, Lord, as coming
from Thy hands. I know that it comes in
blessing, for I am Thine, as Thou art ever
mine.

8. CONTENTMENT

CONTENTMENT has been said to be the supreme virtue. Contentment means living to the fullest the good of every passing moment. Above all, it means living *behind* the present moment, in the Eternal Now.

How much is lost in life by people who perennially wish things other than they are! who complain unceasingly, and tell themselves that the world owes them more than it is giving them!

We must smile inwardly with God, knowing that life is His dream. Contentment is the surest way of drawing the very best out of every circumstance.

Affirmation

Through life's mightiest storms, I am contented, for I hold in my heart God's peace.

ঽ

Prayer

Lord, as You live eternally at rest in Yourself, so let me live also, contented ever, that I may be worthy of living in Your joy.

9. DEVOTION

NO GOOD END is ever reached without devotion. No true success is achieved unless the heart's feelings are involved. Will power itself is a combination of energy and feeling, directed toward fulfillment.

In the quest for God, the unfolding of the heart's natural love, in the form of deep devotion, is the prime requisite for success. Without devotion, not a single step can be taken towards Him. Devotion is no sentiment: It is the deep longing to commune with, and know, the only Reality there is.

Affirmation

With the sword of devotion I sever the heart-strings that tie me to delusion. With the deepest love, I lay my heart at the feet of Omnipresence.

ஐ

Prayer

Beloved Father, Mother, God: I am Thine alone! Let others seek Thee — or seek Thee not; it matters not to my love for Thee. Through all life's trials, my prayer is this alone: Reveal Thyself!

10. FORGIVENESS

FORGIVENESS IS the sword of victory! When we forgive those who seek to hurt us, we rob them of their very power to do us harm. Better still, if they respond with love, they will unite their strength to ours, and so our strength becomes doubled.

But forgiveness should not be given primarily for its effect on others, but rather for the freedom it affirms in our own hearts. Let no outward circumstance condition your inner happiness. Be not pleased merely when man is pleased. Be pleased, rather, when you feel God's pleasure in your heart.

Affirmation

All that befalls me is for my good. I welcome
any hurts that I receive as opportunities to
grow in understanding.

ૐ

Prayer

Lord, how often the hurts that I've sustained
in life have grieved me! Strengthen my
power of love, that I surrender all things to
Thee, my eternal Friend.

11. WILL POWER

WILL POWER, and not the vague abstraction *luck*, is the secret of true achievement. Will power, on subtle energy levels, generates what only looks like luck, by magnetically attracting to us opportunities. Our will is strengthened by removing from our minds the "no-saying" tendency: the obstructions of doubt, of laziness, and of fear — yes, even of the fear of success!

Will power is developed by persevering to the conclusion of whatever one attempts. One should start first with little undertakings, then proceed to bigger ones. Infinite will power comes from harnessing the little human will to God's infinite, all-powerful consciousness.

Affirmation

My will is to do that which is right to do. Part, all you mountains that stand in my way! Nothing can stop my progress!

❧

Prayer

O Infinite Power, I will use my will, but guide Thou my will in everything I do, that it reflect Thy will.

12. SELF-CONTROL

IF A LAKE is made to feed into too many streams, it will soon become drained. Similarly, if a person's heart energies are fed into countless streamlets of desires, he becomes drained, eventually, of even the power to feel. Sated with pleasure, he grows dry, blasé, and indifferent to even the greatest wonders.

The sensualist imagines that by giving up his pleasures he would renounce happiness. But in fact, the more one restrains his senses and learns to live in the peace of the inner Self, the more he finds himself glowing with happiness, good health, and a radiant sense of freedom and well-being.

Affirmation

I am strong in myself. I am complete in my
Self. The joy and perfection of the universe
await discovery within my inner being!

❧

Prayer

I crave nothing that the world can give me,
Lord. O Infinite Perfection, make me one
with Thee!

13. PATIENCE

"PATIENCE," it has been well said, "is the shortest path to God." To attune the heart to the rhythms of Eternity, one must first adjust himself to life's longer rhythms. He should not allow his mind to become absorbed in concentration on the little ripples at the surface of the sea.

Patience means also adjusting to whatever *is* in life, rather than wishing it were something else. Patience is a prerequisite for every type of success. For it is when we work with things as they *are* that we can change them to whatever we might like them to be.

Affirmation

I am neither the ripples at the surface of the sea, nor yet the crashing waves: I am the vast ocean deeps, unaffected by mighty surface storms, untouched by any superficial change.

❧

Prayer

Long have I called Thee, Lord, but Thou hast not answered me. Ah, but for what long eons didst Thou endure my fickleness! In this life, Lord, and if need be through eternity, I will keep calling Thee!

14. GOOD HEALTH

GOOD HEALTH IS MORE than the state of not being ill! It is a radiant state of inner well-being.

Physical illnesses may be cured by medicines. No medicine, however, can induce that state of boundless energy which comes when every cell in the body cooperates with the mind willingly, joyfully in all that it seeks to do.

Such radiant well-being comes after the mind has been cleared of every shadow of unwillingness, of fear, and of doubt; when one has learned to say *yes* to life; and *when one has learned to love.*

Affirmation

My body cells obey my will: They dance with divine vitality! I am well! I am strong! I am a flowing river of boundless power and energy!

❧

Prayer

O mighty Source of all that is right and good, help me to see my strength as an expression of Thy infinite power. Let me banish the darkness of disease: It is forever foreign to Thy light!

15. ENTHUSIASM

ENTHUSIASM IS the spirit of joy channeled through the power of the will. If we want to know joy, we must live always in the full expectation of it. Not even earthly happiness can come to those who demand it glumly, or who work for it with their eyes to the ground. To achieve happiness, one must work with happiness. To achieve divine joy, one must be keenly enthusiastic in everything one does!

Never presume. Never brush aside that subtle feeling of doubt which attends false, emotional enthusiasm. Try always to let God's joy express itself through you. Thus, your enthusiasm will grow, eventually to become His joy!

Affirmation

In everything I do, my enthusiam soars to embrace infinity!

≈

Prayer

O Perfect Bliss! Guide me, that I express Thee through my every feeling. May my enthusiasm be a channel for Thy joy.

16. WILLINGNESS

WILLINGNESS MUST BE cultivated deliberately. It is an attitude of mind, and depends not on outward conditions.

Most people are willing or unwilling depending on their likes and dislikes. This habit tends to develop a bias toward unwillingness, which gradually becomes chronic, and attracts to itself chronic failure.

Don't wait for favorable circumstances to awaken willingness in you. Train yourself in the attitude of saying *yes* to life! Often by this simple attitude you will find Success arriving, unexpected, at your door!

Affirmation

I welcome everything that comes to me as an opportunity for further growth.

❧

Prayer

Lord, help me to overcome the satanic pull of unwillingness. The more I embrace life in Your name, the more I feel Your joy.

17. HUMILITY

HUMILITY IS NOT self-deprecation; it is self- forgetfulness! It is knowing that God alone is the Doer. It is the realization that nothing in this shadow-world of appearances is all that important, except as it draws us closer to the Lord.

Never tell yourself that you are sinful, or weak, or incompetent, or lazy, except as such a statement may help you to surrender joy-fully to God's power. Then *live* by that power! Never wear the mask of false humility. Humility is self-acceptance, and self-honesty. You have a right to all power if you seek it in Infinity, and if you never hold the thought that it resides in your little self.

Affirmation

I live by Thy power, Lord. What I have is ever Thine — ever Thine!

≈

Prayer

Thou art the Doer, Lord, not I. Express Thy perfection through me, as I strive ever eagerly to live in Thy light!

18. COURAGE

THERE ARE three kinds of human courage: blind, passive, and dynamic. Blind courage doesn't count the cost until it finds itself faced, horror-stricken, with the bill. Passive courage is the strength of will to adjust to reality, whatever it may be. And dynamic courage is the strength of will not only to accept reality, but to confront it with another reality of one's own making.

There is a fourth kind of courage: not human, but divine. Divine courage comes from living in the awareness of God's presence within, and in the realization that He is the sole Reality. Live more in Him, for nothing and no one can touch what you really are.

Affirmation

I live protected by God's infinite light. So long as I remain in the heart of it, nothing and no one can harm me.

≈

Prayer

I look to Thee for my strength, Lord. Hold me closely in Thy arms of love. Then, whatever happens in my life I shall accept with joy.

19. SERVICE

SERVICE IS ennobling. It is a way of offering our human littleness into the great Reality that is God.

Service should not be given with the thought that one is serving people, merely. It should be given with an inward consciousness to the Lord who resides in all creatures. When we serve others in this spirit, we find our own spirits becoming freed from egotism. Peace then fills us, in the realization that there isn't anyone with whom we need compete.

What joy, to think that we belong to God!

Affirmation

I will serve God through others, and by my service to Him release the hold the ego has on me. I am free in God! In God, I am free!

❧

Prayer

All that I do, Lord, I do for love of Thee. Accept the flowers of my service to Thee as I place them on Thy altar of omnipresence.

20. INCOME

MONEY SHOULD be seen as an energy-flow, not as something that can be hoarded. For when money is treated as a material reality, it blocks one's creative flow.

Money, like matter, is only frozen energy. Energy is what creates matter. It is energy that forever moves, changes, and dissolves matter. Matter, untouched by energy, is inert.

If you need to increase your income, know that the energy you put out is more important than specific schemes for earning. Energy will *attract* opportunity. Recharge your energy from its cosmic Source, and whatever income you need will be ever yours.

Affirmation

The treasury of the Infinite is mine, for its wealth is energy, and *I* am energy!

≈

Prayer

O Mighty Fountain of Infinite Light, from whose spray the countless galaxies are made: Let me wash away my worldly ambitions in Thy waters. Let me bathe in radiant eddies of Thy energy. Thou art my wealth; Thou, my Treasure; Thou, my Security!

21. KINDNESS

WHEN YOU can view all human beings as members of your own extended family — your brothers and sisters, mothers, fathers, and children — then you will find wherever you go that love awaits you, welcomes you! It is God who gazes back at you, when you behold Him in all!

Kindness is the recognition that all are truly our own. Kindness comes from not minding how others feel about us. It comes from the simple understanding that kindness is its own reward, worth giving out to others, because the source of so much sweetness in ourselves. For those of broad sympathies, the very universe is home!

Affirmation

The whole world is my home, and the human race, my family. With God's kindness I embrace all men.

❧

Prayer

Divine Mother, help me to see that by kindness to others I attract not only theirs in return, but Thy kindness as well. May I be kind to others always. May my kindness act as a channel of Thy unselfish love.

22. TRUTHFULNESS

TRUTHFULNESS IS NOT caustic statements of unpleasant facts and unflattering opinions. Such statements are usually born of pride. But truthfulness is the effort always to see the *divine* truth behind appearances. It is the effort to express always that aspect of truth which may prove the most beneficial.

Truthfulness, as applied to ourselves, means not to hide behind self-flattering justifications: to look honestly at our real motives for doing anything, and not to flinch before unpleasant realities in ourselves. Truthfulness means seeing things as they really are, but then looking more deeply for ways to improve those realities.

Affirmation

Whatever is, simply *is*; I cannot change it for the mere wishing. Fearlessly, therefore, I accept the truth, knowing that, at the heart of everything, God's truth is always good.

❧

Prayer

Heavenly Father, I will not fear the truth, for I know that Truth comes from Thee. Help me to see behind all appearances Thy smiling, all-compassionate gaze.

23. INTROSPECTION

PEOPLE commonly delude themselves with easy rationalizations. "Maybe I wasn't as kind as I might have been," they'll say, "but wouldn't you have been unkind, too, if he'd treated you that way? It wasn't my fault. The fault was his." Thus, the blame for every wrong is placed at one's neighbor's door.

Introspection means to behold oneself from a center of inner calmness, without the slightest mental bias, open to what may be wrong in oneself — not excusing it, but not condemning, either. Introspection means referring what one sees to the superconscious mind, and detachedly accepting guidance, when it comes.

Affirmation

I am what I am; wishing cannot change me.
Let me therefore face my faults with gratitude, for only by facing them can I work on
them, and change them.

❧

Prayer

Let me not delude myself with desires, Lord.
Teach me to see behind the play of my
thoughts Thy ever-calm gaze of wisdom.

24. CALMNESS

CALMNESS IS perfectly achieved when life's little wave becomes absorbed into the cosmic sea, in divine ecstasy. In daily life, too, we can achieve calmness to a degree by keeping our awareness focused on the reality of the Spirit underlying all outward circumstances.

Calmness comes with the determination to live ever happily in the present moment, relinquishing the past, and not worrying about the future, but placing our lives firmly in God's hands, and knowing that He is fully in command. Calmness comes with non-attachment — with knowing that nothing in this world is truly ours.

Affirmation

Though the winds of difficulties howl around me, I stand forever calmly at the center of life's storms.

֍

Prayer

With Thee beside me, I know that the tides of trouble can never sweep me away. Hold fast my hand, Lord; never let me go!

25. PEACE OF MIND

PEACE of mind is the result, not of money in the bank, but of prayer and meditation. The more one contacts God in meditation, the more he feels descending upon him a blanket, as it were, of inner peace, cooling his body, calming his restless impulses, and thrilling his nerves with ever-new delight. Peace is like a weightless waterfall, washing away all worries, and bestowing a new, glad sense of confidence.

Peace of mind is his who knows that God is his only Treasury!

Affirmation

From pools of inner silence I sip the sparkling waters of Thy peace.

ɤ

Prayer

All that I own is Thine, Lord. Help me to know Thee as the River of Peace, running silently beneath the sands of my life's experiences.

26. NON-ATTACHMENT

NOTHING is ours. No one belongs to us. Mentally, we should make a bonfire of our love for God, and cast into it all attachments, all desires, all hopes and disappointments.

It helps mentally to examine one's heart every evening, and liberate it anew of all desires. Pluck out from your heart any burrs of new attachments that you find clinging there. Cast them joyfully into the fire of devotion.

Pray to God energetically, "I destroy all my attachments. They are no longer mine, Lord. I am free in Thee!"

Affirmation

Nothing on earth can hold me! My soul, like a weightless balloon, soars upward through skies of eternal freedom!

ॐ

Prayer

I destroy all my attachments. They are no longer mine, Lord. I am free in Thee!

27. CONSIDERATION FOR OTHERS

CONSIDERATION for others is one of the marks of a refined spirit. Many people on the spiritual path feel that, since it is within that they are seeking the kingdom of God, and since they are working at developing a spirit of non-attachment, it doesn't matter how they express themselves to others. Indeed, their inconsiderateness is an affirmation of their independence of the opinions and feelings of others. "If God is pleased," they tell themselves, "what matters the displeasure of man?"

Yet by unkindness we can never please God, who is all Kindness itself. Sensitivity to others is a way of self-expansion. One truly achieves freedom in himself when he can respect their realities, because he is wholly at peace with his own.

Affirmation

By sensitivity to others' realities, I keep myself in readiness to perceive the truth no matter what garb it wears.

≈

Prayer

Divine Mother, I worship Thee in all Thy forms, both ignorant and wise. Finding Thee within, may I behold Thee enshrined in omnipresence.

28. DISCRIMINATION

AS SCIENCE judges the relative speed of any object by one constant, the speed of light, so the devotee judges the relative merit of any idea by the one constant, God. Discrimination is clear only when it relates everything to the Eternal Absolute. Thus, while the intelligence may toy with ideas endlessly, discrimination asks, "Is this wisdom? Is it of God?"

True discrimination is not even the product of reasoning. It is soul-intuition. Reasoning, even from the highest point of reference, is uncertain compared to the inspirations of superconsciousness. To discriminate clearly, meditate first. Ask God to guide your understanding.

Affirmation

Resolutely I quell my inclinations, that my mind be open to the wisdom-guidance of my soul.

❧

Prayer

Guide me, Lord, that in all things I know Thy will, for I know that only by Thy will are all things led to perfection.

29. RENUNCIATION

RENUNCIATION MEANS turning one's back on non-essentials, that we may give our whole attention to the Lord. We might think of renunciation as an investment, which initially may seem a loss, but in time becomes multiplied to many times its original worth. The least gift that we give to God will return to us, in divine blessings, a thousandfold. Renunciation means nothing less than the gift to God of oneself.

Renunciation is of the heart. It isn't what you wear, or the outward rules you follow. When you renounce all for God, you hold that renunciation as a precious secret between you and Him. All your desires, all your ambitions, then, are for Him alone.

Affirmation

I spurn the tempting magic of this world,
with its rainbow bubbles, ever ready to burst.
See where I fly: high above the tall mountains. I am free! I am free!

ॐ

Prayer

Lord, help me to see that in no outward
experience will I ever find fulfillment. All
that my heart has ever sought awaits me in
Thee.

30. NON-INJURY

NON-INJURY is a fundamental rule in the spiritual life. It means primarily an attitude of mind. Outwardly, one cannot avoid doing a certain amount of injury — for example, to flying insects when driving one's car. The harm one does, however, by wishing harm to others hurts not only them, but even more especially, oneself. Spiritually, a harmful attitude separates one from the harmony and oneness of life.

Non-injury, on the other hand, embraces that oneness, and is in turn sustained by it. Non-injury is a powerful force for victory, for it enlists cooperation from the very universe, where harmfulness incites endless opposition.

Affirmation

I send out the rain of blessings to all, that love be nourished in hearts that, heretofore, have known only hate.

*

Prayer

Divine Mother, when others seek to hurt me, give me the wisdom to see that victory lies in blessing them, not in revenge. If I respond with anger, the loss will be mine, even if mine also is the outward victory, for inwardly I will have been hurt indeed. But if I return blessings for their blows, I shall remain ever safe within the impregnable walls of my inner peace.

31. CONCENTRATION

CONCENTRATION is the secret of success in every undertaking. Without concentration, thoughts, energy, inspiration, purpose — all one's inner forces — become scattered. Concentration is the calm focus of one's full attention on the purpose at hand. Concentration means more than mental effort: It means channeling your heart's feelings, your faith, and your deep aspirations into whatever you are doing. In that way, even the little things in life can become rich with meaning.

Concentration should not involve mental strain. When you really want something, it is difficult *not* to think about it! Concentrate *with interest* on whatever you do, and you will find yourself absorbed in it.

Affirmation

Whatever I do in life, I give it my full attention. Like a laser beam, I burn from before me all problems, all obstructions!

❧

Prayer

Help me to see Thee, Lord, as the Scriptures describe Thee: "the most Relishable"! Help me to concentrate on Thee my gaze, my love, my aspirations, my entire being.

32. SELF-EXPANSION

SELF-EXPANSION IS the essence of all aspiration. Why do we seek to possess things? Because by acquisition we imagine we'll expand our dominion. Why do we seek to learn more? Because we think by enlarging our knowledge to expand our understanding. And why do we seek ever new experiences? Because we believe that, through them, we'll expand our awareness. When you stretch a lump of dough outward, it becomes not only broader, but thinner. Such often is the case when we stretch the mind only outwardly. Reaching out too far, we sacrifice depth in our lives.

The Self-expansion toward which all life aspires is of the spirit: an expansion of sympathy, of love, of the awareness that comes from sensing God's presence everywhere.

Affirmation

I feel myself in the flowing brooks, in the flight of birds, in the raging wind upon the mountains, in the gentle dance of flowers in a breeze. Renouncing my little, egoic self, I expand with my great, soul-Self everywhere!

❧

Prayer

Beloved Spirit in all that is! Help me in my own nothingness to find myself one with all that is.

33. GENEROSITY

MOST PEOPLE THINK of generosity as merely the giving of material benefits to others. More important, however, and much more satisfying is a generous spirit: a willingness to let the other person shine, even if it means being eclipsed oneself; a happiness in his good fortune, even if it means personal loss for oneself; a concern for his safety, even if, in an accident, one's own property has been destroyed.

Generosity means, above all, recognizing that everything we have and are belongs to God alone, and is His to dispose of where He will.

Affirmation

I am happy in the good fortune of all, even more than in my own, for in my happiness for them lies inner freedom.

ॐ

Prayer

All that I have and am is Thine. Divine Mother, dispose of it as Thou willst.

34. ALERTNESS

THERE ARE two currents in life: One takes us downward toward unconsciousness; the other, upward toward cosmic consciousness. The first is an impulse born of the sense of past familiarity. Life, like a lotus, evolves out of the mud of lower consciousness toward the light of divine awareness. Subconsciously, we imagine ourselves comfortable with the stages we've traversed so far, but we are not always so ready for the adventure of further growth!

The second current in life is the soul's impulse. We cannot find happiness in turning back toward the mud. Fulfillment lies only in reaching up toward perfect divine awareness. To achieve it, we must be alert in everything we do. For in the flow of increasing wakefulness lies the joy we all are seeking.

Affirmation

I am awake! energetic! enthusiastic! I give my full, alert attention to everything I do, knowing that in absolute consciousness I shall find God.

❧

Prayer

Let me pray always with alert, awake attention to Thy listening presence, knowing that Thou dost hear the merest whisper of my thoughts.

35. INSPIRATION

INSPIRATION IS of two kinds: the re-discovery, or rearrangement, of thoughts that already exist in the subconscious mind; and the sudden appearance of new thoughts, or new insights, from the superconscious. This higher inspiration, certainly, is more to be desired than the lower, for it is based in truth and not in imagination.

It is not always easy, however, to recognize the difference between lower and higher inspiration, particularly when the lower is vitalized by the emotions. When inspiration comes, receive it with calm love, and see whether, untouched by emotion, its impulse grows stronger or weaker. Love is the water that nourishes true inspiration.

Affirmation

I hold my thoughts up to the calmness within; in calmness I receive inspiration from my higher Self.

❧

Prayer

O Spirit, Thou art all truth. In Thee lies the solution to my every need. Inspire me now, Lord! Show me which path to follow of the many that lie before me.

36. POWER

POWER IS an aspect of God. Human beings often associate the word *power* with ruthless ambition and dominance over others. But it is a misdirection of power to exert it over others for selfish ends, and a misuse of it to exert it without care for their well-being. Rightly understood, power is the ability to command our own energies — above all for our own transcendence, but also for the good of others. Such power is important for spiritual growth.

Many people imagine that spiritual development is manifested as a sort of saccharine sweetness. The saints, however, are people of enormous inner power, before which others often tremble! Yet theirs is a power only for good. Its roots lie buried in the soil of pure love.

Affirmation

Mine is the power of the universe, channeled for my own awakening and the awakening of other sleeping souls!

❧

Prayer

Help me to feel that Thy power runs through my veins, courses through my thoughts, and sets my noble feelings afire with love for Thee!

❧

37. WISDOM

WE OFTEN HEAR the expression, "sadder but wiser." This is the mark of worldly wisdom, which people equate with disillusionment. Indeed, worldly hopes, sooner or later, all end in disappointment, and sometimes in great sorrow. Worldly wisdom often wears the garb of sadness.

Not so, divine wisdom! On the spiritual path, the expression should be, "happier and wiser"! For true human wisdom means recognizing at last the pathway *out* of delusion, and toward the light of truth.

Divine wisdom is Omniscience itself. In such wisdom there is no shadow of sorrow, only bliss absolute, bliss infinite, bliss eternal!

Affirmation

As I learn the lessons that life teaches me, I grow toward ever-greater joy and freedom.

❧

Prayer

I am grateful, Lord, for every test You send me. Each time I stumble, help me to learn. Each time my human weakness makes me fall, help me to grow stronger. May I realize behind every pain Thy calm, reassuring wisdom.

38. JOY

TRUE JOY is not an emotional state. It is not that which one feels when some desire is satisfied, or when everything at last goes well. It is inward; it is of the soul. It can be developed, first, by not reacting emotionally to outward things.

Don't be tossed on alternating waves of success and failure. Don't join, in their excitement, the buyers and sellers in the marketplace of this world. Be calm in yourself, even-minded and cheerful through the gains and losses of life. Then, in calm, deep meditation feel the joy of the soul. Hold on to that joy through all activities. Don't confine it, but try ever to expand it, until your little joy becomes the joy of God.

Affirmation

I am even-minded and cheerful at all times. I
know that joy is not outside me, but within.

ઢ

Prayer

In the calmness of meditation, at the heart of
my inner peace, help me to feel Thy thrilling,
joyful presence.

39. SELF-CONFIDENCE

SELF-CONFIDENCE, as it is normally understood, recalls to mind images of army generals and cowboy heroes — people, in short, who know their blacks from their whites. But life's alternatives are usually much more complex.

Self-confidence on the spiritual path is of another order altogether. It means confidence in the inner Self, not in the ego. It means living from within, living by truth rather than by opinions. It means living by what God wants, not by what man wants. Thus, it means living by faith, in the sure knowledge that, although man is fallible, God is infallible.

Affirmation

I live in the assurance of God's truth within.
In my inner Self, and not in the opinions of
others, lies true victory.

ૐ

Prayer

What matter, if people blame me? Of what
importance is their applause? I live to please
Thee, Lord, confident that when Thou art
with me I am protected, though it be from an
enemy horde.

40. AWARENESS

AWARENESS deepens, the more it is centered in itself. But the farther a person's interests extend outside himself, the thinner the supply line of his awareness becomes.

If a person's consciousness is centered outwardly in things, it takes on those qualities which it attributes to those things. Jewellers, for instance, often have bright eyes. People with no sense of higher values have dead eyes. Man needs to learn to change his focus from what he is aware *of* to what he is aware *with*. He needs to become more aware *at the source* of his awareness, at his deepest center, God. Through this awareness, his enjoyment even of the surrounding world becomes intensified a thousandfold.

Affirmation

I behold the world with eyes of calmness and of faith. For I know that, as I view others, so will I myself become.

ప

Prayer

Infuse me, from my deepest center, with Thy joy. Make me aware of Thee, my divine Beloved, in all that I behold.

41. POSITIVE THINKING

AS WE think, so we become. And as we think, so our lives and circumstances become also. From the divine consciousness come answers to all our questions, and solutions to all our problems. It is in lower consciousness that confusion reigns.

Think positively in everything you do, for in that way you help to attune yourself to the divine flow. One who is inwardly in tune with grace finds all things harmonious and beneficial being attracted to him. Positive thinking, combined with the sense of divine attunement, is never presumptuous, for it draws its power, not from the ego, but from the consciousness of God's joy within.

Affirmation

My outer life is a reflection of my inner thoughts. Filled with the joy of God, I express His joy and harmony in everything I do.

৵

Prayer

Problems cannot exist, Lord, whenever Thou art near. Give me strength always to hold Thee in my heart.

42. HUMOR

A GOOD sense of humor is an effective means of keeping a sense of perspective through the trials and difficulties of life. By not taking things too seriously, one develops non-attachment.

One should not laugh too much, however, lest the mind become light, and one's view of life, superficial. Thus, one needs to achieve a sense of perspective where humor itself is concerned. The best way to do so is to share one's laughter with God; to laugh with the sense of *His* joy, within. Never laugh at people, but rather *with* them. For humor should be kindly, not sarcastic. Laugh with pure delight, and everyone will join you in your laughter.

Affirmation

In laughter I recall my own mistakes. Merriest am I when, by laughing, I include myself!

☙

Prayer

I delight in life's comedy, for it reminds me that true sanity exists in Thee alone!

43. EVEN-MINDEDNESS

MANY PEOPLE confuse progress with movement and with outward change. Thus, the more dust of excitement they can stir up, the more productive they feel they are! The more they get swept up into a happy mood when things go well, the better, they imagine, things have gone. And their answer to every slump is to cast about for some other thing to sweep them high once more. Such lives are like cars driven over deeply rutted roads: Their movement is almost as much up and down as it is forward.

With even-mindedness, progress is a straight, not a jagged, line. Progress, however, should mean above all progressive understanding. Even-mindedness bestows clarity of perception, which is the ability to see things as they really are, undistorted by emotional bias.

Affirmation

I remain untouched by gain or loss. In the calm mirror of my understanding I behold Thy light reflected.

‌‌‌‌ઽ

Prayer

When I rejoice, Lord, let it be with Thee. And when I grieve, help me always to see Thy sunlight through the mists.

44. ACCEPTANCE

ONE OF the most difficult lessons in life is to learn to accept things as they are. How much energy we waste in trying to wish away the inevitable! "If only this hadn't happened!" "If only we had reached there in time!" The "if only's" and "might have been's" in life keep us from dealing realistically with what *is*.

Acceptance comes from knowing that reality lies within ourselves, and that all else is a dream. Acceptance of that one reality makes everything else acceptable. Instead of learning to come to grips with a thousand individual challenges, therefore, make the supreme effort to accept God unconditionally into your heart. Accept all that comes in life as coming from His hands. He will give you what is best for you, if you live for Him alone.

Affirmation

I accept with calm impartiality whatever comes my way. Free in my heart, I am not conditioned by any outward circumstance.

ॐ

Prayer

Shine Thy delusion-cauterizing light into the hidden nooks of my heart's feelings, lest somewhere, without my conscious knowledge, I have not accepted Thee. If ever I err, strengthen me to accept Thy discipline, for in Thy will alone lies the happiness I am seeking.

45. OPENNESS

OPENNESS CAN BE a great virtue, but only when it is exercised with discrimination. To be open to wrong ideas, or to people who would harm you, would be foolish. For it is not with openness that error can be conquered, but with love.

Openness of mind is a virtue when it is centered in the desire for the truth. Openness of heart is a virtue when it is centered in love for God. Both mind and heart, however, need filters to screen out what is not true, and what is not of God. This we can do by referring back for approval to the divine presence within whatever comes to us. We must be ever open to truth and to God, but ever closed, or at least indifferent, to error and delusion.

Affirmation

My mind is open to the truth, whatever its source. True statements remain valid, even if hurled in anger.

ه

Prayer

Divine Mother, let me hear Thy melodies everywhere: in the laughing brooks, in the songs of nightingales — yes, even in the roar of city traffic! Behind all earthly sounds, let me listen for Thy voice alone.

46. MORAL VIGOR

LACK OF moral vigor saps the will, and makes the intellect sponge-like, ready to absorb the prevalent opinion of the times. People with good intellects often suffer from the "Hamlet complex": the inability to come to any decision, or to commit oneself to anything. They justify their indecision by saying, "I want to be fair to all sides." But even an imperfect action is better than no action at all.

When you believe in something, stand by it! When you believe in someone, stand by him! Such loyal self-commitment is a higher law than "seeing all sides." Energy is needed to accomplish anything in life. With moral vigor all things are possible. But without it, the end of every act is failure.

Affirmation

The decisions that I make in life come from within myself, from my sense for what is right. I am committed to the truth, and to channeling it outward to the world.

ॐ

Prayer

Divine Mother, with every action of my will let me express Thy divine vitality, Thy truth, Thy perfection. Let me live to serve Thee alone, or else die in the attempt!

47. PERSEVERANCE

"LOYALTY," my great spiritual teacher used to say, "is the first law of God." Most people are fickle. They change their jobs, their spouses, their friends, their beliefs, their ideas — not because of any new expansion of awareness, but because they lack the simple power of perseverance.

One must be loyal to one's principles, and not allow oneself to be ruled by sentiment. To be loyal to others, and to one's assumed goals in life — not for sentimental reasons, but in the name of principle — is the way of divine progress. Perseverance can be difficult, for in every undertaking there is a certain amount of dull routine. Don't be ruled, therefore, by likes and dislikes, but do whatever has to be done. If it is right, let *nothing* intervene until the job is finished.

Affirmation

I will finish what I set my mind to do before
leaving it for something else. My word is my
bond. So also is my resolution.

☙

Prayer

Though the sirens of distraction call me to
turn aside and relax the sternness of my
dedication, keep me steadfast on my path,
Lord. My goal in life is Thee!

48. GRATITUDE

GRATITUDE IS a way of returning energy for energy received. Only a thief takes without paying for what he gets. And one who accepts a kindness without returning gratitude, as though the kindness were his by right, demeans both the giver and himself. He demeans the giver, because by ingratitude he implies that the kindness was inspired by selfish motives. And he demeans himself, because by giving nothing in return he breaks the cycle of creativity, without which prosperity's flow, both materially and spiritually, is blocked.

Accept nothing, inwardly, for yourself, but offer everything to God. Don't let yourself be bought by others' kindnesses. Be grateful to them above all in your soul, by blessing or praying for them. Give gratitude first of all to God, from Whom alone all blessings truly come.

Affirmation

I give thanks to the giver behind each gift, and to the one Giver behind all that I receive. My gratitude rises with devotion's incense to the throne of Omnipresence.

જ

Prayer

I thank Thee, Lord, for all Thy blessings. But most of all, I thank Thee for Thy love.

49. IMMORTALITY

YOU ARE NOT your body. You are not your thoughts, your desires, your changing personality. Your body has a certain age, but you, yourself, have no age! Your body may tire or become unwell, but you yourself, the fatigueless soul, cannot tire, can never know disease!

Tell yourself always, "I am a child of eternity!" Don't be identified with your outward form, nor with change, but live in timelessness. It is our identity with change that creates the illusion of passing time. Feel that, through all outward changes, you, the immortal soul, remain the same. Death itself will be but one more change; be not identified with it. Then, when death comes, you shall rise in eternal freedom!

Affirmation

I am a child of eternity! I am ageless. I am deathless. I am the changeless Spirit at the heart of all mutation!

❧

Prayer

Wherever my body travels outwardly, let me feel Thy changeless presence within. Wherever my thoughts take me, let them return always, like prodigal children, to find repose in Thee.

50. PRACTICALITY

MANY spiritual seekers, and others with high ideals, lose sight of the need to make their idealism practical. Many even resent the suggestion that they try to put an ideal into practice — as though the very effort to do so would mean somehow lessening its purity!

But God is no idle dreamer! Were the universe not kept in a state of perfect balance, chaos, not harmony, would be the common state. We, too, should be practical in our idealism. Life, to be ever expansive, must be a search for truth. "Will it work?" is the preliminary question to, "Is it true?" The test of an ideal is whether it is practical or not. By practicality, we mature from the state of idle dreaming to become emissaries of the truth.

Affirmation

Though my spirit soars in the skies of consciousness, my feet and hands labor here on
earth to make truth real to all.

ಶ

Prayer

Let not my thoughts lift me up through beau-
tiful clouds of imagined possibilities, unless
You give me the power also to materialize my
dreams.

51. GOD-REMEMBRANCE

TO REMEMBER God means not only to think of Him constantly, but to realize that finding Him is an act of remembrance truly. For it is from Him that we have come. When the clouds of delusion evaporate from our minds, what will be left is what was there always, hidden behind the clouds: the blazing sun of divine consciousness!

One should not strain, nor reach outward mentally, to think of God. Know that He has been yours always — nearer than your nearest thoughts and feelings, nearer than the very prayers you offer Him! Think not merely *about* Him: Think *to* Him. Share with Him your passing feelings, your idlest fancy. Talk *with* Him. Practice His presence — at first, perhaps, for minutes a day, then for hours, and then all the time.

Affirmation

I will live in the remembrance of what I am in truth: bliss infinite! eternal love!

ॐ

Prayer

Lord, Thou art always with me. Help me to feel, behind my thoughts, Thy inspiration; behind my every emotion, Thy calm, all-transforming love.

52. HIGH-MINDEDNESS

PEOPLE OFTEN speak of cynicism as the mark of realism. In fact, in a universe without any visible center, one might justifiably develop his understanding of it from any conceivable starting point. One's understanding, however, will only reflect who and what he himself is. A view from the depths lacks the perspective that can be achieved from the heights. From the mountain top, all things are seen in their true proportion.

Strive always to be a channel for high thoughts and inspirations. Never cooperate with anything petty or mean. Remember, the universe is, for each human being, both a mirror and an affirmation. One who entertains high thoughts will be, himself, ennobled.

Affirmation

I will see goodness in everything. I will view the world around me, not from the depths of matter-attachment, but from the heights of divine aspiration.

❧

Prayer

Lord, The universe was made in Thine image of perfection. Help me to bring out that image in others by blessing them in Thy love.

ABOUT THE AUTHOR

J. DONALD WALTERS is a direct disciple of the great master, Paramhansa Yogananda, with whom he lived and studied for 3 1/2 years. For nearly forty years, Mr. Walters has lectured and taught around the world. He is the author of a number of books, among them: *Secrets of Happiness, Secrets of Success, Secrets of Attracting and Keeping Friends, Secrets of Persuasion, Secrets of Meditation, Secrets of Inner Peace, Secrets of Overcoming Harmful Emotions, The Beatitudes – Their Inner Meaning, Rays of the Same Light,* and *The Path,* He lives near Nevada City, California, at Ananda World Brotherhood Village, a spiritual community dedicated to the principles described in this book. For more information, please call or write to the publisher.